Why Should We Save Water?

by Mr. Spicer's class
with Tony Stead

capstone
classroom

With all the lakes, rivers, and oceans on Earth, we seem to be surrounded by water. We also get water from the sky when it rains and snows. But did you know that people can only use about 1 percent of all the water on Earth? With more than 7 billion people on our planet, this is a very small amount of water for cooking, cleaning, and drinking.

Therefore, we need to save water instead of wasting it. In this book, you'll find out why water is such an important resource and why it has to be saved.

Let's Change the World!

A Guide to Using Less Water

by Gia

Have you ever wanted to keep your ecosystem safe? Well, with my information, you can! One way is by saving water. You should be grateful that you have clear, pretty water to drink. There are many ways you can save water.

When you are brushing your teeth, do you leave the water on? You may think, "Huh, it won't take me that long to brush my teeth!" If you do this, then you are wasting water. Turn off the faucet while you brush your teeth to help conserve water.

Another way to save water is to replace your older toilet. Think about it—you may have a mom, a dad, a sister, a brother, and yourself. If you have an older toilet, it is using about 3.6 gallons of water for every flush. A family with five people would use 54 gallons of

toilet water every day if each person flushed three times a day! In a whole year, it would be a lot more:
54 gallons × 365 days = 19,710 gallons. That's a lot! A newer, high-efficiency toilet uses a lot less water.

Every once in a while, everybody wants to take a nice, hot, relaxing candlelit bath in the dark. Even I do! But don't take them too often because you have to fill up the tub. You should evolve from taking a bath to taking showers. Try to avoid taking long showers because, like baths, they waste a lot of water.

We need to keep our ecosystem running smoothly. Conserving water is a start.

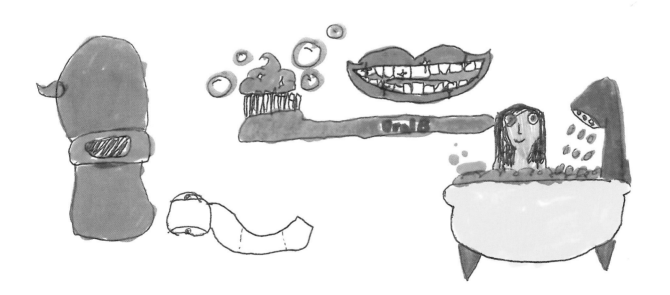

Reduce and Recycle

by Anthony and Josh

Have you ever taken a shower and all of a sudden the water gets cold? That is probably because you have been in the shower too long, and that's not a good habit. Conserving water is very important because water is a precious environmental tool that humans take for granted.

We should conserve water and keep it clean. If we don't, then we won't have enough sanitary water to drink or to bathe in. We should also make sure to recycle because if we throw away plastics and other recyclables, they could get into our drinking water and pollute it.

Water is limited, which means it will eventually run out. In order to help our water supply, people have to find ways to conserve water in their homes. Also, the more water you waste, the more money your family will have to pay in water and electric bills.

It's important to save water because it helps all of us and our environment. Think about ways that you can save water and reduce pollution.

Water Is Important

by Marissa

Water is very important. We drink it, we use it to take a shower, and we need it because it's good for us. I think that we should save water and the world by using less. Using less water will also save us money.

One way to save water is to use a refillable water bottle. You can keep filling it up instead of buying plastic water bottles that can harm our environment. Another way to save water is by turning it off when you brush your teeth. In addition, you can spend less time in the shower. For instance, take a 20-minute shower instead of a 5-minute one. It may help to set a timer. When it goes off, then you know to get out. According to professor Nick Gray's blog, water is renewable only until a certain point.

I read on one website that you can save water in many different ways—you can soak your pots and pans in water and scrub them. You can also run your washer and dishwasher only when they are full.

These are the reasons why you should save water and some ways you can do it.

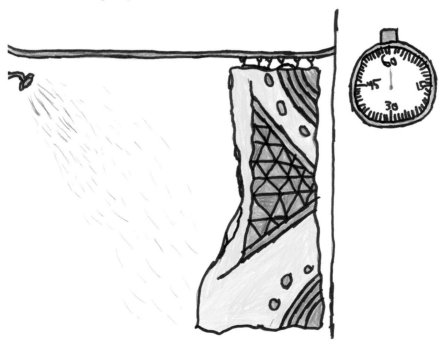

Protect Our Water

by Vann

I think that we should conserve water because it is very important to our Earth and our lives. I will explain why.

Without water, I don't think we could have a human civilization. Every single drink we take and every piece of food we eat would not be possible without water. In addition, energy bills are higher when we don't conserve water. If we don't protect our water sources, we can't power certain things that use water, like water-powered clocks. But most importantly, people, animals, and plants would die if we run out of water by wasting it.

If everyone could do a little to help, we could conserve a lot of water.

Save the Water Cycle!

by Luca

One HUGE reason we should be careful with our water supply is the effect a low water supply would have on the water cycle. The water cycle describes how water circulates on Earth. During Earth Science class, I learned that the heat from the sun is the driving force of the water cycle. Water is something that can't be created by man. Clouds can make snow, hail, rain, and sleet. The four main parts of the water cycle are evaporation, condensation, precipitation, and collection. If we damage our water supply, we will be messing up the entire cycle!

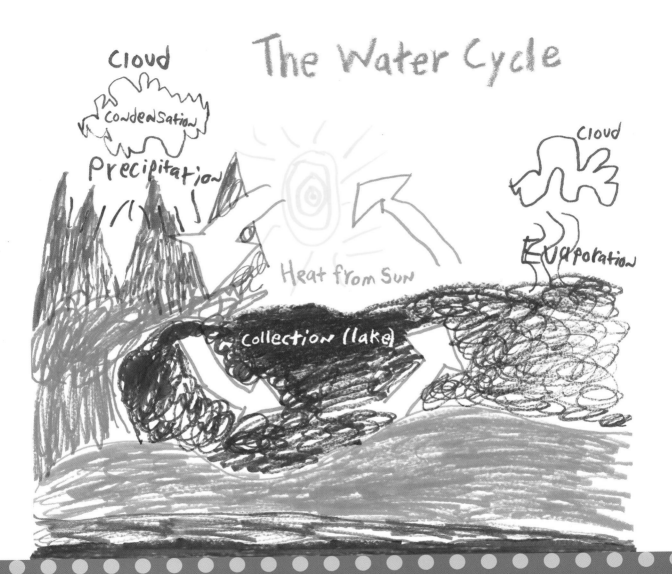

Save Our Water, Save the World

by Eva

In many countries around the world, there is not enough water. Water can be used for many different purposes, including hydration, hygiene, and people's daily needs. Many people take water for granted and don't consider the less fortunate who don't have things, such as fresh water. We need to be more thoughtful about how we use water to help those who are less fortunate.

There is not one human being on the planet who would be able to live without water. We all know that water hydrates our body, but water does many other things; for instance, water carries the nutrients to the cells in our body. Water also removes all the waste products from our cells and helps regulate our body temperature. So as you can tell, having fresh water is crucial to our survival.

Water is not only for drinking. It has many different uses. We also swim, shower, and play in water. But there are places in the world where fresh, clean water is very rare. If we want a drink we can simply buy a bottle of water from a shop or drink it from a tap. But for some people, getting much-needed water means walking a long way to find it. And even then, it's often not clean like the water we have. Instead, it's likely to be filled with nasty diseases and animal waste. Can you imagine getting a bottle of polluted water?

The majority of our planet is made out of water, and for many of us, regular rainfall is a way of life. And yet so little fresh and clean drinking water is available for so many people. Those of us who live with easy access to drinking water need to consider people with no access at all. Otherwise, we are potentially wasting lives every time we waste water.

Keep our world a happy Place!

Water Helps Us Survive

by Alex

I think we need to conserve water because we use it every day. We need water to keep our dishes and food clean. If we run out of water, we can't clean our food or dishes, and we can get sick from food poisoning.

In addition, we need to keep our possessions, like our clothes, clean. If we don't keep our clothes clean, we can get sick from bacteria that are hiding in our clothes.

But most importantly, we need drinking water to survive. We can't live very long without it. This water has to be freshwater, otherwise we can't drink it. Only 1 percent of Earth's water is freshwater that we can use, so our water supply is very limited. Protecting this small supply is very important.

So what are some ways to conserve water? Well, don't leave the tap water running while cooking, brushing your teeth, or washing your hands. Finally, don't run the dishwasher and washing machine until they are completely full with dirty dishes and clothes. More time between washes means more water saved!

Now that you know why we need to conserve water, what will you do about it?

Save Our Water

by Eli

Imagine a world with so little water that it costs more than gasoline. (Currently it's $3.59 for one gallon of gasoline.) Everybody would be thirsty, stinky, and dirty. We need to save our water and keep it clean so our world does not end up like this.

Here are some ways to save water: Turn off the faucet when you are brushing your teeth, take a shorter shower, water your garden only when it needs it, and check for leaks in your water pipes. According to one website, even the smallest leak wastes 20 gallons of water per day! Once we had a leak that we did not know about, and our water bill doubled!

In our Land and Water unit in school, we learned about rain barrels and fog nets. Rain barrels are big buckets that collect the water from gutters. People then use this water for watering gardens and other plants. Fog nets are similar to rain barrels, but they catch fog moisture to make water.

It takes a lot of water to have healthy flowers and gardens. I think making a rain barrel or a fog net is a great idea. I hope a lot of people do this so in the future we still have plenty of clean water!

Ways to Save Water

by Bryan

Water covers about 71 percent of Earth, but we can only use about 1 percent of all that water. Even if you live in an area with ample rainfall, it is important to not waste water. To help save water, you can take a shower for less than 5 minutes, and turn the water off when you are brushing your teeth. According to the United States Environmental Protection Agency, an American home uses approximately 400 gallons of water every day. We can reduce this and save money by conserving water. Never let the water go down the drain when there may be another use for it, such as watering a plant or garden. Brush your teeth first, and then turn on the faucet when you are ready to wash out your mouth. There are many ways to save water. Maybe you already do some of them.

Turn off the water when you are Brushing your teeth

All of the students who wrote this book argue that it's important to conserve water. It helps keep us alive, and it keeps our planet healthy. As part of their research, they found many different ways that you could conserve water and recommend that you:

- Turn off the faucet while brushing your teeth.
- Buy a newer, high-efficiency toilet.
- Take shorter showers.
- Recycle, don't pollute.
- Use a refillable water bottle.
- Run your dishwasher and washing machine only when they are full.
- Make a rain barrel or fog net.

You may agree that we need to save water, but you might have other ideas for saving it. If you had the chance to write the next few pages of this book, what would you say about conserving water?